Reflections
of
Love

Alan Hines

Order this book online at www.trafford.com
or email orders@trafford.com

Most Trafford titles are also available at major online book retailers.

Printed in the United States of America.

ISBN: 978-1-4669-8252-9 (sc)
ISBN: 978-1-4669-8251-2 (e)

Trafford rev. 03/06/2013

Trafford
PUBLISHING®   www.trafford.com

North America & international
toll-free: 1 888 232 4444 (USA & Canada)
phone: 250 383 6864 ♦ fax: 812 355 4082

This book is dedicated to my truest reflections of love, my grandmother Jean Hines (whom are in heaven) and my twin daughters Alantis and Alexis Hines.

Acknowledgements

Special thanks to the heavenly father for giving me life, and blessing me with the talent to write creatively, and for all of his blessings. Special thanks to Jean Hines, Alantis Hines, and Alexis Hines. Special thanks to my mom, and dad, Joyce Hines, and Alan Laughlin for getting together and creating me. Special Thanks to my sister Alicia Hines (Precious) for inspiring me to become an author. Special thanks to President Obama, and the first lady. Special thanks to Julie Hull (attorney) and John Fitzgerald Lyke (attorney). Special thanks to Mr. Marasa. Special thanks to all those that showed me love throughout life. Special thanks to all those that showed me no love; in which motivated me to become more self-sufficient which enable me to flex my full potential in life.

Thanks to the entire Hines, and Laughlin family, Roscell Hines (Cel), Alan White (Block), Shamon Miller (Pac).Thanks to Buferd for helping me get through troublesome times. Thanks to the staff at my job Durable Packaging, my manager Marco (Good Guy), all the Q C's whom are wonderful, and everybody else at Durable that's been so helpful to me. Last but not least thanks to Ricardo Sanchez for being there in my time of need.

Contents

Motivational Speaker

She was a motivational speaker.
A beautiful creature.
A church preacher.
A collector's item as a keeper.
Had me conveying things that were deeper.
A person for the people.
Caring as a sequel.
Against injection that was lethal.
Studied the history of her Black people.
Treated everyone as an equal.
Wasn't concerned about midevil.
Spreaded her love like the wings of an eagle.
In a good way she motivated the people.

Beauty Was Her Name

Beauty was her name,
she put ancient women and today's super models
    to shame.
Her frame was a reflection of her beautiful name.
Her skin possessed not a bump or even a stain.

Beauty was this lady's name,
as she should be placed in the hall of fame.
Outta one sight, men came.
Beauty within her couldn't be contained.

Beauty was her name,
as she'd maneuver as that outta a movie
    screen . . .
Someone out of a magazine . . .
Beauty was a queen.

Sexy Lady

She walked as she was listening to music grooving
    to a beat.
For she was the light of the streets.
This sexy lady must be from some foreign
    country.
She talked without profanity, how discrete.
Smiles of pearly white teeth; even her feet are
    pretty.
She's a sexy, sexy lady!

Lift My Head to Jesus

I lift my head to Jesus,
as if it's a significant meaning of life being
  pleasing.

I lift my head to Jesus,
as he loves us, for our sins he bleeded.

I lift my head to Jesus,
as the devil has no meaning.

You Don't know My Name

You don't know my name,
but to me you're like a flame.

My heart screams your name.
Each time you pass inside I plead for you to be
    my main.
As your image haunts my brain.

You don't know my name,
for that I complain.

Please tap into my brain.

You don't know my name,
but for you I'll do anything.

Light of the Day

She moved with such style and grace;
she was the light of the day.

She had a way that amplified the poems she
conveyed;
the light of the day in her own special way.

She had a stylish way,
in which the things she'd say would light up
each day in a distinction way.

Just her expression would get her paid.

She began to specialize in the fixing of the entrees;
self-made recipes of making others have better
days.

She was the light that shined throughout the
day . . .
the light of the day.

My Claim to Fame

Hey, Ms. Thing, you are my claim to fame.
Without thee, obscurity would be my name.

My claim to fame allows the sun to shine
    through the rain.
Stimulates my brain.

Ms. Thing, my life wouldn't be the same,
without the fame you claim . . .

Let Me Take You For A Ride

Let me take your entire mental capacity for a ride.
A ride where cruise ships and luxury cars coincide.
A ride where homicide doesn't reside.
A ride where people of all ages will slip and slide.

Let me take you for a ride,
where no cats but humans will have nine lives.

Let me take you for a ride,
where peace will be multiplied.

God Delivered Me From Evil

God has delivered me from all evil.
The devil has no sequel.
No doings of illegal.

As leading us not into temptation will be
meaningful.

For I possess no racism,
we're all God's people and shall be treated as
equal.

God has delivered me from all evil,
simply because he loves his people.

I'll See You Next Time

I'll see you next lifetime,
because you're faithfulness is dying.

I ask where were you last night,
as you continue lying.

I'll see you next lifetime,
as your love is blind.
Your domestic abuse is inclined.

I'll see you next lifetime,
but I hope you remain fine.

Found Time

I finally found the time to enchant your mind
    with this civilized rhyme.
Within this rhyme you must read between the
    lines;
as our affection simultaneously combines.

I found time to create this systematic rhyme,
to express my feelings for your mind.

Although I've known you almost half my lifetime;
I finally found time and courage to write this
    rhyme,
as a love letter designed.

British Katrina

She spoke with a British accent,
it was evident that she should run for president.
Heaven sent, a womanly prince.
Spiritually inclined and content, utilized common
    sense.
British Katrina and I was meant.

My Love and God

I Loves God and I know he Loves me.
His kindness is forever with me.
He gives me rest and walks beside me.
His ways in safety always will keep me safe as
    I can be.
He is a good friend, not an enemy.
His love is with me for all eternity.
My love for thee will always be.

A Love Story

For my story be that of love, because of her . . .
She was 6'9 and gorgeous enough to give sight
to the blind.
For her, but only her, I'd travel back in time.
Her religion forbidden her not to eat swine,
yes she was holy and divine.
For as she talked each word rhymed.
Her hazel eyes would allow the sun to shine.
Her kisses were as sweet as she was fine.
Her body was shaped better than a dime.
Her style was different but yet and still was less
of time.
Each time she'd come by I'd smile.
For I really want her to give birth to my first
child.

Brown Skin

I love your brown skin.
I think of it every now and then.
As sun rays blend in your brown skin is a
     spectacle designed just for men.
Your brown skin is the atmospheres best friend.
Ebony descendants, I love your brown skin
     every now and then.

Please Forgive

Please forgive me for not acknowledging your
    presence.
For not treating you as a princess.
For not saying how much I love your tender
    caress.
For not being more appreciative to God's gift
    to men . . . women.

Please forgive me again and again.
To me you're more than a lover and a friend.

Please forgive me for not showing love from
    the beginning to the end.

For She Is

For she is the one that makes cats have nine lives.
The one that gives me new life.

For she is the reason why I'm still here.
She always help me to bring in the new year.

She is in demand.
Groovy and grand.
She is a woman.

The Girl Named Alice Nicknamed Al

This girl name Al, its as she copied my style.
As I travel to see her my journey last a long while.
Inside she drives me wild.
A lover and a pal.
Got me considering walking down the aisle.
The cutest in any crowd.
Autopsy should never be filed of this girl
    named Al.

This Girl Janet

This girl Janet must be from another planet.
This girl Janet is a love bandit.
Makes me feel splendid.
Makes my life be more understanding.
She just gotta be from another planet . . .
    Janet.

I Had A Friend

I knew you when I had a friend.
As sunny days begin with no end.
From the city of sin.
Women . . . a man's best friend.

I knew you when I had a friend now and then.
For when I'm confined in around many men,
from a distance I always had a friend, women.

Some content to involve with domestic violence;
as a man I could never bring eminent danger to
    a womanly friend.

As my world seems to come to an end,
through you it has just begin.

The tenderness of ten.
My one and only genuine friend.
A precious gift to men . . . women.

The Body of Genet

Genet has a body that would make the sun sweat.
People with Alzheimer's wouldn't forget.
Within a swimsuit had no stretch marks or
regrets.
The body of Genet should win each and every
pageant.
Flawless, as men imagined about Genet's fashion.

Come to Town

Everytime I'd come to town she'd come to see
    how I got down.
She adored my poetic sounds.
All the other poets she'd heard was clowns.
Pleased when I came to her town,
love having me around,
wanting me to make my home in her town,
so she could always hear my sounds.

Mallery

This female named Mallery was a showcase
    like an art gallery.
She changed falsehood to reality.
Through her there will be no affectional
    technicality.
With Mallery I'd like to one day build a family.
This female named Mallery could have access
    to my salary.
She was my cure from allergies.
In the night we'd create formality . . . Mallery.

Under a Spell

I'm under a spell by the influential lady named
    Michelle.
This spell makes me feel well.
It's the best spell that I can mention about, or
    tell.
This spell shall not be undid and remain sterile.
She got me under a spell in which brings color
    to pale,
size to frail, and breath as I exhale . . .
    Michelle.

Apart

For when we're apart you'll remain within my heart.

Mentally for you I designated a special place that won't be burglarized,

or set firely sparks;

for your body I'll guard.

I never wanna be apart;

simply because your love shines even in the dark.

The finding of another you would be hard.

Never wanna depart, apart.

Jew

Her eyes was the color of blue.
Ethnic origin was that of a Jew.
She made dreams come true.
She was like an action pack movie coming to a
    theater near you.
She was like a tamed animal at a zoo.
She was the reason why they knocked down
    the Berlin wall,
where freedom was due.
This feminine Jew.

Seductive

She was so seductive;
mastered the art of loving, kissing, hugging,
and cuddling.
Seductive, her loving was more beneficial than
tons of gold or money.
Sweeter than honey.
Nothing could compare to her seductive way
of loving.

Elaine

My fame came through this great dame, Elaine.
Around my house its hundreds of pictures in
frames, faces of Elaine.
I glorify her name, and anything she had became.
My personal game was gained through this
dame better known as Elaine.
The inventor is the one to blame of Elaine's aim,
which was to please my grain.
What she'd bring couldn't be changed.
Authenticity bottled up with no drain.
Even in my second life I'd always remember
her name . . . Elaine.

Treason

For her I committed treason.
Political Science I didn't believe in.
She was the realness that never changes
throughout the seasons.
She was the only reason why I'd ever commit
treason.
She was the truth as I believed in.
She was hot and steamy.
Goodness naturally breeding . . . .
For her I'd committed treason.

To Light, To Light

She brought things to light as sky rockets in
    flight.
She'd give the dead new life.
She brought things to light as our love affair
    was the definition
of being correct and right.
She brought things to light that I couldn't
    imagine seeing with
my own sight; at least not in this life.
She brought things to light.

Reason Why I Sing

It's a reason why I sing, your amorous is what
you bring.
The bearer of delightful things.
Sweetness of a dream.
Glorious for you I sing.
I sing as freedom rings.
You're the reason why I sing.
You're the meaning of clean as your love shines
like a beam . . . .
The reason why I sing.

She Made Things Clearer

She made things clearer as signs of the end
    wasn't getting nearer.
Showed me good spirits as reflections in the
    mirror.

She made things clearer as my love for her was
    cushioned like a pillow.

With other women, no love will be revealing.

Clearer as my destiny was to be a spouse and a
    father of children.

She made things clearer.

Isn't She

Isn't she lovely, isn't she wonderful.
She's something like a miracle.
So beautiful.
She's the one that makes hearts glow.
Something like a picture made by Picasso . . . .
Isn't she wonderful.

She Got

She got an authentic genuine beauty, oh what a cutie.

She gots an appealing learning ability as a college student.

She got a profound way with words.

She got a way to get her message heard.

She got a great imagination.

She got a character that needs no replacement.

Something About You

It's something about you that makes me smile
instead of frown.
Something about you makes me mentally wear
a crown.
Something about you makes me never want to
leave town.
Something about you that makes the earth go
round and round.

She Took Me

She took me to this special place to show.
She taught me how to rhyme using a poetic
flow.
Throughout time she and I continued to grow.
She always gave me the green light to go.

She took me to this place to show that I've
never been before.
In this place to show down below she was like
a futuristic super hero;
everything there she controlled.
She dictated the pace as she did things to make
me love her so.
Her love is all I wanna know.

She took me to this special place to show,
and I'm still here from ten years ago . . . .
This lovely place to show.

The Genuine Love of My Life (My Daughters)

6-26-96 began a new era of love within my life, because of your birth.

For my sins you shall not be cursed.

Without you living life wouldn't be worth.

I thank God, Doctors, and the Nurses for your birth;
as my love for thee will forever be disbursed.

Even When No One Else Cares (Alicia Hines)

Even when no one else cares you have always
    been there.
Even when my world was at an end you have
    been a friend.
There's others whom have played a role in the
    safeguard of my life;
but you are the number one delight.

I'm No One Without You
(Alicia Hines)

I'm a nobody without you . . . .

Without you my respiratory system would be
    suffocated in the midst of seclusion.

Without you I couldn't see the fullness of moons,
there would be days filled with gloom,
my life would be doomed.

Without you my body would be decomposed
    to shreds.
I'd permanently have stress within my head.
That's why I'll love you even when I'm dead.

Butterfly Affect

As this butterfly affect begins to play with no
    reset or no eject.
It'll be the realist love ever met.
Love being exercised without breaking a sweat.
Like a subject that won't have a test.
It's the best of all the rest.
Feels better than anything at it's climax.
A new name for no stress.
This butterfly affect I'd never forget.

Loving You Is Easy

Loving you is easy simply because you are
    beautiful,
and the way you treat me I know the feeling is
    mutual.

Loving you is wonderful,
better than an artifact or show.

Loving you is easy because you allow me to
    grow.

This Girl

This girl rules my world.
She can rearrange peace out of turmoil.

This girl is like the sun after the rain.
This girl can turn crazy men sane.
This girl must have my last name.

Life Guard

A lifeguard that made living life easy instead of
    hard.
Saving lives was planted in her heart;
if need be she'd even swim through sharks.

Deep within I never drowned in her parts;
she made me feel like a Greek God.

Each second with no end as it starts, lives she'd
    guard.

This Destination

As I reach this place and destination it'll be
loving instead of hating.
Smiles will be enhanced on faces.
Body parts will permanently be stationed,
as I reach this final destination.

It's Hard to Hide

It's hard to hide what I feel inside.
Internally I joyfully cry.
For you are my inspiration and pride.
You bring the truth to love without a lie . . . .
It's hard to hide what I feel inside.

Fantastic

She was fantastic, far from average.
Lived life lavish.
Promised satisfaction.
Peaceful and relaxing.
Moved forward without backtracking.
Love that had no destractions.
Genuine like leather, instead of plastic.
She loved fashions.
Talked properly within linings.
All things she did and the way she carried
herself was fantastic!

My Time Wasn't In Vain

My time wasn't spent in vain.
I read thousands of pages worded with your
    name.

My time wasn't spent in vain as each second,
your frame remained as it came.

My time wasn't spent in vain as I attended college
studying the core of your brain;
love I gained.

My time wasn't spent in vain as the solar system
provides rain, people and times change, my love
for thee will remain the same . . . .
Never in vain.

Best

She was my road to success.
An A+ on every test.
A tender caress.
She was truly blessed.
Even better than all the rest.
That's why after her, there will be no next.

Fortune and Fame

Some people live for fortune and fame.

Well for me, I remain the same plain as Jane.

My fame came through this unique dame;

She eases brains as I claim you as my infinite
fortunate fame.

For you I'll never change.

Through slick rhymes I'll recite the best game.

My love will be for you to obtain as fortune
and fame.

Across my heart I'll tattoo your name: Fortune
and Fame.

Inner Emotions

My inner emotions for you come out.
You be the judge of my love without a
reasonable doubt.
I glorify your name from my mouth,
from north to south.
Within my emotions you have clout.

Made My Day

She made my day, each day.
When she came around I'd always remain
    speechless with nothing to say;
smiling her way.
Please by her enchanting array.
She made the sun shine my way even on a
    rainy, or Winters day.

Each and every day she made my day in an
    indifferent,
but beautiful way.

I See You and Wanna Be You

I see you and I wanna be you.

Your words speak the mere truth.

You're like an action packed movie coming to
a theater near you.

As a critic . . . Golden Globe awards are long
overdue.

For you be the reason why I feel brand new.

Romance Story

For this non-fiction story will consist of love;
Tilted The Romance of Doves That Was.
For endless chapters shall be because,
because our love always is, and was.
For this story will depict the heavens up above;
no violence, no hurricanes, nor floods.

Faithfully our story shall be that of love.

Smiles

I see the way you smile that shows me you and
I shall one day create a love child;
with the probability of walking down the aisle.
I see the way you smile, lovely as can be, but
yet and still mild.
I see the way you smile as hearing not guilty
verdict in trial.
Even when I'm not around hearing my
name brings you to show off your stylish
smile . . . .
I love to see you smile.

Loneliness as It Seems (Dedicated to women who have been in bad relationships)

Loneliness as it seems.
Those that have dated only interested in sex or
    schemes.
My inside internally bleeds.
My hunger for genuine love would someone
    please feed.
My days of love I plead.
Unhappy I be, someone rescue me.

Faithfully I be the individual you want me to be.
I do what it takes to make you happy;
I never lie or cheat.
But your heart rapidly increase, full of deceit.

I need someone to love me for me.
To be my love to be.

Loneliness, I'm tired of thee.

Just For Me

Just for me you've prepared loving extensively.
Just for me you perform forbidden intimacy.
Just for me you've planted a seed that will
    grow for many centuries.
Just for me you're devoted to being lovely as
    can be . . . .

But all these things are only, "Just for Me."

Please Believe

Please believe that my warm attachment will
   always be.
Within captivity I express words of relief,
setting inner feelings free.

Please believe that my heart will reach until
   affection is complete.

Please believe that I'll love thee until doctors
   and coroners meet.

Isn't She Marvelous

Isn't she marvelous?

Isn't she the one that permits intelligence within the retards?

Isn't she marvelous like the artwork of a dead artist?

Isn't she marvelous as the creator whom created Mars?

Isn't she marvelous enough to be one of the shining stars?

For We Shall Shine

For we shall shine in time as happiness and
    love combine.
Where intimacy, intimately will be the place to be.
Where our minds will be regulated by sweet
    dreams.
Where loving is what it seems.
As you and I will be Kings and Queens.
Your body will be my love thing.
Ecstasy hot as steam.

For we shall shine and gleam more than anything.

For we shall shine as being supreme.

Part of Me

Part of me wants you to stay.
The other part wants to leave.
Although you cheat your love is still received.
Through our kids happiness is achieved.
For thee will always be a part of me until the
earth's core bleeds.

I Can't Stop Thinking of You (Ladies)

I can't stop thinking of you and all the things
you do.

Your voice is that of keys to a piano.

Some wear jeans and tennis shoes.
While others wear heels and skirts.
I love each one for what it's worth.
Ladies first.

I think of you while you're here, and when
you're not around.
I think of you no matter the area or town.
I think of you even as my life goes down.

I Love You All (FEMALES)

For I love you all, big, tall, or small.
For I love you all as my membrane roams your
    halls.
I love you all as the state of being un-paused.
I love you all as your age, location, or ethnic
    origin has no cause.

For I truly love you all.

Love to Your Mind

I want to make love to your mind,
as we mentally climb a vine.
As your heart, mind and body will eventually
become all mine.

In time, I'll find the perfected rhymes to entertain
your mind.

As within lines they'll be no manipulation signs;
your mind will be satisfied.

My soothing words will stimulate your mind at
all times.

Once I have seized possession of your mind
everything that yours will become mines.

Shining, Ms. Cherry

You've shined your light upon me.
I want the world to see how lovely Ms. Cherry
can be.

As I'm in solitude you set me free; free from
misery,
for you're the true essence of happy.

As you provide me with climax that's greater
than the rest.
For you are truly blessed.

Who knows what the future will unfold but I
pray that the Lord will bless your soul.

As you grow old, I'll be there because I really
do care.

As people, places, and things change I'll remain
the same.

Because of you I'll refrain, refrain from all bad
things.

Ms. Cherry, I want the world to know your
name.

MOM

She will always be my favorite girl.

The conqueror of my world.

Gave me life, like, as I was her quality diamond and pearl.

Showed love to me even throughout the incident with Lil Dearl.

I still remember back in the days when she wore the Jerry curls.

When Dad wasn't around I still was hers . . . .

My favorite girl in the world.

For You

For you I'd go to war and sacrifice my life in battle.

For you I'd jump off a tall building knowing I can't fly.

For you I'll flight a thousand professional boxers.

For you I'll give up my religion to become an alcoholic.

Can you Be Mine

Elegant lady can you be mines until civilization
    declines?
Can you be mines through the changing of
    seasons and throughout times?

Can you be mines in a special intimate way?
Can you be mines every second of the day?

Love to Be

Her love came from a fruit, an apple from a tree;
how sweet she can be.
She kept me away from harms obscurities.
She was the best I could see.
Made my life complete.

My love to be kept our love affair high as can be;
higher than ecstasy.

She created a value in me that let me be me . . . .
She was my true love to be.

The Love of My Life (Daughters)

For you be the love of my life, although you
   can never
actually be my wives.

The love of my life I thank the higher power I
   met your mom on that rainy night.

The new love of my life your birth took me to
   paradise, gave me new life;
as all future decisions will be made right!

The love of my life I see heaven on earth in
   your eyes.

The love of my life was born on the 26th, a
   month before July.

Bells

Let her name ring bells . . . . Michelle.
With stories to tell;
As she'll tell them well.
Pleasing an audience, she shall never fail.

Bells mixed with her scent of Jamaican cash
    crop to smell.

Bells as the coming of daylight will be realistic,
but something like a fairy tale.

Bells that will bring opposite genders together
    for each others heart to feel.

Bells that will be heard on top of hills.

Everyone ears will be anxious to hear Michelle's
    bells.

Bells that the Medical field will use to heal.

People of all walks of the earth will yield to the
        power and authority
of Michelle's bells.

Greek

The Greek Goddess of rain.
Kept me sane.
Gave me all her brain.
Constantly we'd fly to Spain.
She was my main.
Cultural difference wasn't a thing.

Her rain would feed me soil for growth and less
    pain.
Loving sustain, flowing through my veins.

I'm glad she came.
She's sweet as sugar cane.
My everything . . . .
The Goddess of rain.

Became

She became a part of my silent mind.
I'd think of her all the time.
Sometimes it'll be fantasies and past experiences
    combined.
Other times she was like a tool in my head that
    eased my mind,
help me get through troublesome times; my sun
    that shined.

She was just so fine.
Remind me of Cleopatra in her prime.
Female monarch from the beginning to the end
    of time.

She finally became mines.

She Don't Care

State of caring.
Luring, provocative, and daring.
Considerate when it came to sharing.
Child bearing.
Natural beauty, couldn't stop staring.
Treat people as equals, never comparing.

Of my flaws she didn't care.
Her features continuously remained glaring,
as she was truly caring.

Who is Her?

Who is her? For she is me and I am her.
Who is her? She is the inventor of the word love.
Who is her? She is the cutest lady ever.
Who is her? She's a female from another planet.

Sweetest Lady of Them All

Sweetest lady of them all, I address to you this
    missive in hopes
of it serving a purpose for your cause; to be
    respected as the
sweetest lady of them all.

Sweetest lady of them all, you create an
    atmosphere that has no flaws.

Sweetest lady of them all, your sweetness will
    never pause.

Your finesse consists of your own little set of
    laws.

Sweetest lady of them all.

Rocked the Mic

She rocked the mic, a standing ovation show.
Had a secret recipe got the audience wanting mo.
Anchor, anchor, as we all enjoyed her flow.
We never wanted her to go.

I was checking her out on the low.
A showcase from head to toe.

Acappella needed no instrumental.
Voice would crack bullet proof windows.

Stalked her, even changed my zip code.

To good to be true must be a ghost.

Astounding with her lyrical flow.
Rock the mic for sho like a musical hero,
and kept me wanting mo.

Shall, Time

In time you shall shine like an Aurora.
In time you shall stand victorious.
In time you shall be a notorious historian whom
    will
write glorious stories.
In time you'll be with no worries . . . .
Only in time.

Earthly Lady

This love was meant to be.
My earthly lady this earth is design for you
and me.

As we swim through seas seeing sights of
blossomed green leaves,
earthly lady you and I can be.
Can be part of the air people breathe, the oxygen
lungs need, food for thought that feeds;
even those full of greed.
We should be the H20 that people want and
need.

Places we land, people never wants us to leave.

No harm to bleed.

The love of loves to be . . . .

My earthly lady, you and me.

Governor of My World

For you be the governor of my world;
older woman or younger girl.

For without you us men couldn't even be born
    fertile.
The governor of my world is a creation that's
    worthy to respect as loyal.

She should never have to work a job or feel
    labor pains.
I praise all thy names.

If you ever need a friend you can depend on me.
The governor of my world, in which I see.

She Told Me

She told me things to be,
from the date of birth and even when I'm past 53.

She told me that one day the blind would see,
prisoners would be free, and she and I would be.

She told me that one day she and I would rule
the country,
dictate the economies money, and that I
shouldn't trust buddy.

She told me things to be, as she gave me this
crystal ball to see . . . .
She told me.

Different

We was from two different walks of earth.
She was from the surface;
as I was mentally buried under the dirt;
until I met her in a skirt.
A Registered Nurse.
Creative in the way she'd flirt.
Throughout our love affair I never got hurt.
She laid a foundation as I was her turf.
Alone and in public we showed our love off for
    what it was worth.
Amongst the citizens we'd hold hands, and I
    even carried her purse.
She made things clean outta dirt.
I did what I could to give her new life as birth.

Although from different walks of the earth our
    love
connection still worked!

Intended for Me

My lady that was intended for me.
You're delicately lovely, sweet, shaped petite.
You make my life complete.
I've roamed the streets endlessly, someone
    like you
I'll never meet, even if my life repeats.
You were intended for me positively.

I Just Can't, Without You

I can't do, without you.
You be the nutrition of fruit, meetings of group,
    respect that's due.
It'll be no life on earth without you.

As winds that blew.
As melodies flow from flutes.

Without you, suicide would be long overdue . . . .
I just can't without you.

LOOKS

If looks could kill for you I'd die a thousand
    times.
Skin smoother than a new borns back side.
When around I never wanna close or even
    blink my eye.
I wish your beauty could always be nearby.
I can't lie you're the cutest alive.
I always find a way to look at you on the sly
    admiring
the gift you are to the human eye.

Do She Loves Me

She loves me, she loves me not.
Even when I sneeze my heart won't skip a beat
or stop loving she.

Sometimes I wonder if she loves me or not . . . .
Or if she's in love with the currency I got.
Do she loves me or not, or is she more interested
    in the
sports car I drive.

Do she really love me, or not;
either way my loving for her won't stop.

Unbroken Hearted

Unbroken hearted, dearly departed, I love you
regardless.
Even if you turned crippled or retarded.
Gray hairs, access weight but yet and still
marvelous.
Because of your figure you'll be a man's target.
No matter what happens I love you
regardless . . . .
Broken hearted, dearly departed.

She Had

She had a way with words that was absurd.
The way she spoke played tricks on my nerves.
More intelligent than a nerd.
Spoke loud so her poetry could be heard.
She was like a definition as she defined words.
Spoke in a way that mentally had me soaring
    with the birds . . . .

She really had a way with words!

Journalist

She was a journalist that wrote in a journal
of my life in a list.
A bliss, lips to kiss.
Released my fist as peace sits;
as I told her my life story, even the secretive
     events.

Felt as if I could convey to this
journalist my historical evidence.
I told her everything in my life that
ever existed . . . .

This journalist.

Lady from Mars

I'm wishing on a star to follow where you are,
lady from Mars.
I'm wishing for a star that travels from earth to
    Mars;
this star is the love of ours, freedom behind
    bars,
oxygen we will breathe even on Mars,
this lady from a far.
Lady from Mars.

Common Interest

For you, I have a common interest that's evident
that you and I was meant.

Time shall be spent as realness won't bend.
I'm interested in being a lover and a friend.

We shall be together like conjoined twins.
For we share a common interest.

Live Again

You allowed me to live again,
cleanse me of all sins, defined the definition of
    a friend.
The rebirth of a new man.
Continuous love that never ends.
Made me feel young again.
I live again, and again, and again.
Never shall be six feet within.
I live again scars turned to baby skin,
problems never begin.
I live again because you brought new life in . . . .

This Special Place

Lets go back to this special place,
where past history of skeletons will be erased.
Love written all over your face.
As I'll chase in search of love and taste.
Never forsake and remain in good grace . . . .
In this special place.

Wake Me Up

You wake me up inside . . . . before you, it was
  as another
soul crawled in me and died.

Visions of suicide no longer reside.

You brought true love in my heart in mind.

No more cries, wiping eyes, you've woke me up
  inside.

A Sincere Love Letter

You cross my mind and I decided to drop you
    a few lines.
To me, you're the greatest of all times.
Your visual appearance stays on my mind.
You're the reason I shine.
I truly love you heart and mind.
You're one of a kind.
Another you I could never find.
You be the love of mines.

I Can't Resist

I can't resist to crave for the tenderness of your
     kiss . . . .
The sweet mint.

I can't resist to think of you with a degree of
     evident content.

For I can't resist to treat you as a female Monarch
until times end.

Call Your Name

Heavenly father, I call upon your name.
Forgive me for my sins, not the devil, but I'm the
one to blame.
I call upon your name to proclaim you as the
only King of kings.
I call you name alone or in public with no shame.
Heavenly Father because of you, I'm sane.
I'm a product of all things you've created.
I call your name highly as a soaring plane.
I call your name.

Black and Blue

When no one else loves you that means I do.
A female black and blue.
The essence of true.
Colorful as the colors black and blue.
Someone old and new.
Anything for you I'll do.

Black and Blue.

Still Is

You are and still is the woman of my peers.
Smiles with no tears.
You was and still is the one I always want near,
my dear, sincere.
Still is through the years.
The woman with a vivid vision with no
smear . . . .
Still is here.

Married Wife

Lock doors now open.
Smoothly coasting, expressing inner emotions.
Love runneth over.
Remaining sober.
Faithfulness, other women it's over.

No more staying out late nights,
respectful to my wife.

Genuinely the love of yours and mines.

Clouds (Jean Hines)

Although you hover in heaven above the clouds,
one day . . . . one day I'm going to make you
    proud.

Church members of crowds will holler your
    name out loud,
as they'll mentally visualize your appearance
    smooth skin color of brown;
remembering 2941 W. Harrison church musical
    sounds.

Momma was your title and crown.

Crowned queen on earth as it mound.

Scriptures was never found but we all know the
    creator
cast you down to spread his word and love
    around towns.

Your sight was astound.
The sweetest lady by the pounds.
Genuine that could never be matched or found.
Was the wisest woman around.

From the clouds as not rain but your love runs
    down.

You may contact the author at
ALAN_HINES@yahoo.com
with any feedback or inquiries.